ELVIS PRESLEY

THE LITTLE KID WHO GREW UP TO

BE THE KING OF ROCK AND ROLL

STEPHEN FIELDER

This Book Belongs to.....

_____

COPYRIGHT © 2024 by STEPHEN FIELDER

All rights reserved. No part of this publication may be reproduced, distributed, or transmitted in any form or by any means, including photocopying, recording, or other electronic or mechanical methods, without the prior written permission of the publisher, except in the case of brief quotations embodied in critical reviews and certain other noncommercial uses permitted by copyright law.

Trademarks and pictures are used without permission. Use of the trademark is not authorized by, associated with, or sponsored by the trademark owners. All trademarks and pictures used within this book are used with no intent to infringe on the trademark owners and only used for clarifying purposes.

TABLE OF CONTENTS

GROWING UP IN TUPELO

Discovering Music

The Power of Gospel

Meeting the King of Rockabilly

Recording His First Hits

HEARTBREAK HOTEL AND BEYOND

The Ed Sullivan Show

The Elvis Phenomenon

From Singer to Actor

Serving His Country

Coming Back Stronger

The Las Vegas Era

A Glittering Lifestyle

A Timeless Talent

The King's Farewell

Elvis: A Global Icon

Keeping the Music Alive

Glossary: Music Terms

Elvis-related Vocabulary

Elvis Dance Moves

Quiz Time!

INTRODUCTION

*O*nce upon a time, in a little town called Tupelo, Mississippi, there lived a boy named Elvis Presley. Can you imagine that? A little boy who would one day shake the whole world with his music!

Elvis was born on a cold January day, in a tiny house. His family was poor, but they were filled with love. His mama, Gladys, sang beautiful lullabies to him. His daddy, Vernon, worked hard to make ends meet.

Elvis loved music from the very start. He'd listen to the radio for hours, tapping his feet and singing along to the tunes. He loved the sound of the blues, the rhythm and the feeling. It was like magic to him.

Elvis had an amazing voice, a voice that could soar like an eagle. He'd sing in church, his voice filling the room with a special kind of joy. People would stop and listen, amazed by the sound of this little boy.

Nobody knew it then, but that little boy with the big voice was about to change the world. He was like a tiny seed, planted in the heart of the American South, just waiting for the sunshine to help him grow. And he did!

Can you believe that this little boy from a small town would become the biggest star in the world? Let's follow Elvis's journey and see how it all began...

CHAPTER 1: GROWING UP IN TUPELO

Tupelo, Mississippi, in the 1930s was a world away from the glitz and glamor that would later surround Elvis Presley. It was a place of cotton fields, dirt roads, and a strong sense of community. Here, in a small wooden house, Elvis Aaron Presley was born on January 8, 1935.

His home was modest, but it was filled with love. Elvis's mother, Gladys, was a gentle soul with a beautiful singing voice. She often sang lullabies to young Elvis, and it's believed that these early musical experiences laid the foundation for his future career. His father, Vernon, was a hardworking man who faced many challenges, including a stint in prison for a minor crime. Despite these hardships, the Presley family was united by their deep faith and a strong work ethic.

Elvis was a curious and energetic child. He loved to explore the woods surrounding his home, searching for adventure and imagining himself as a cowboy or a soldier. His imagination was as vast as the Mississippi sky. He was also drawn to music. He would spend hours listening to the radio, captivated by the sounds of the blues and country music.

A turning point in young Elvis's life came when he received a guitar as a gift for his thirteenth birthday. It was a humble acoustic guitar, but it opened up a new world for him. He spent countless hours practicing, trying to mimic the guitar solos he heard on the radio. His fingers ached, but his determination was unwavering.

"I'd sit there for hours, trying to figure out how to play those licks," Elvis recalled later in his life. "It was like learning a new language."

Elvis's musical talent began to blossom. He would perform at local gatherings and school events, his voice filling the air with a raw energy that captivated his audience. People started to notice the young boy with the golden voice. His music teacher, Mae

Moore, recognized his potential and encouraged him to join the school choir.

It was in the church choir that Elvis truly discovered the power of his voice. The gospel music he sang there would become a cornerstone of his musical style. The passion and emotion he poured into these hymns were unlike anything his peers had heard before.

"Gospel music was the real foundation of my music," Elvis often said. "It was the spirit that moved me."

As Elvis grew older, his fascination with music deepened. He would spend his allowance on records, building a collection that reflected his eclectic taste. He loved everything from country to blues to pop. His room was a shrine to his musical heroes, with posters of Hank Snow, Jimmie Rodgers, and Carl Perkins adorning the walls.

These early years in Tupelo were formative for Elvis Presley. They shaped his character, his values, and his love for music. Little did anyone know that this ordinary boy from a small town would go on to become one of the most iconic figures in the history of music.

Discovering Music

Elvis was a little boy with a big secret. He loved music more than anything! Music was his playground, his best friend, and his escape. It was like a magical world he could dive into whenever he wanted.

Way back when, before Elvis was even old enough to tie his shoes, he'd sit by the radio and listen to the music pour out. It was like someone was whispering secrets into his ears. There were songs about love, heartbreak, and dancing. Elvis loved to dance! Even as a tiny kid, he'd wiggle and shake to the music, making his family laugh.

One day, Elvis heard a song that made his heart skip a beat. It was a blues song, slow and sad, but with a beat that made you want to move. The singer's voice was like velvet, smooth and deep. Elvis didn't know it then, but that song was the start of a lifelong love affair with music.

"Music was my first love," Elvis would later say. "It was something I could always turn to."

Elvis's mama, Gladys, had a beautiful singing voice too. She'd often sing him to sleep with soft, gentle songs. Elvis loved to listen to her. He'd try to copy her voice, making silly sounds that made his mama laugh.

"Elvis was always singing," Gladys would say. "He had a voice like an angel."

As Elvis grew older, his love for music only grew stronger. He'd spend hours listening to the radio, trying to figure out how the songs were made. He'd tap his foot, clap his hands, and sometimes even dance around the room.

His favorite thing to do was to pretend he was a singer. He'd grab a broom and hold it like a microphone, singing his heart out. He'd imagine himself on a big stage, with people cheering and clapping.

Elvis's imagination was as big as the sky. He dreamed of a world filled with music, where he could sing and dance and make people happy. Little did he know that his dreams were about to come true.

The Power of Gospel

Elvis grew up in a world filled with faith. His family went to church every Sunday, and the church was the heart of their community. It was a place of joy, hope, and powerful music.

Elvis loved going to church. He loved the singing, the clapping, and the feeling of being part of something bigger than himself. The gospel music filled him with a special kind of energy. It was like a fire burning inside him, making him want to sing louder and stronger.

The church choir was where Elvis really found his voice. He loved to sing with the other kids, their voices blending together like a beautiful rainbow. But there was something special about Elvis's voice. It was stronger, richer, and filled with a raw emotion that touched everyone who heard it.

"Elvis had a gift," said the church choir director, Miss Minnie Mae. "His voice was like an instrument, pure and powerful."

When Elvis sang gospel, it was like his heart was pouring out. He closed his eyes and let the music take him away. He could feel the spirit moving through him, filling him with a sense of peace and joy.

"Singing gospel made me feel like I was flying," Elvis later said. "It was like I was connected to something bigger than myself."

The people in the church loved to hear Elvis sing. They'd clap their hands and shout "Amen!" when he hit a high note. It made him feel proud and happy.

Elvis learned more than just singing in church. He learned about love, forgiveness, and the importance of having faith. These values would stay with him for the rest of his life.

The church was more than just a place of worship for Elvis. It was his first stage, his first audience, and the place where he discovered the power of his voice. It was a foundation that would shape him into the star he would become.

CHAPTER 2:

THE MEMPHIS MOVE

Life in Tupelo was sweet, but for the Presley family, it was also tough. Times were hard, and finding work wasn't easy. So, when Elvis was thirteen, his family decided to move to Memphis, Tennessee, a city buzzing with energy and opportunity.

Imagine leaving everything you know, your friends, your school, and your favorite spots. It was a big adventure for young Elvis. Memphis was a whole new world, full of tall buildings, shiny cars, and people from all walks of life.

The move was tough at first. Elvis missed his friends and the familiar sights of Tupelo. But he was also excited about the new possibilities. Memphis was a city of music, with a thriving music scene. It was like moving to a candy store for a music lover like Elvis.

Elvis and his family lived in a small apartment, but it was a world away from their little house in Tupelo. The city was noisy and busy, but it was also full of life. Elvis loved to explore the streets, soaking up the atmosphere. He'd spend hours hanging out at the local record stores, discovering new music and dreaming of the day when he could make his own records.

One day, while wandering around, Elvis stumbled upon a record store called Sun Records. It was a small, unassuming place, but it was about to change Elvis's life forever. Inside, he heard a sound that made his heart race. It was a new kind of music, a mix of country and rhythm and blues. It was raw, energetic, and unlike anything Elvis had ever heard before.

Little did Elvis know, this was the beginning of his journey to becoming the King of Rock and Roll.

Meeting the King of Rockabilly

Sun Records was like a magical kingdom to Elvis. The moment he stepped inside, he felt a spark ignite within him. The air was filled with the sounds of guitars, drums, and voices, creating a vibrant, electric atmosphere. It was a place where dreams were born and legends were made.

The man behind the magic was Sam Phillips, a visionary record producer with an ear for talent. He had a knack for finding raw, authentic sounds and turning them into gold. Elvis was drawn to Phillips' energy and passion. There was something about the man that made Elvis feel like he could conquer the world.

Elvis spent countless hours hanging around Sun Records, soaking up the music and trying to make connections. He was determined to get Sam Phillips to listen to him sing. But it wasn't easy. There were plenty of other talented musicians trying to catch Phillips' attention.

One day, while working as a truck driver, Elvis decided to take a chance. He gathered his courage and walked into Sun Records with his guitar. He asked to see Sam Phillips, his heart pounding with excitement and fear.

"I can sing," Elvis told Phillips, his voice barely a whisper.

Phillips looked at the young, shy boy and raised an eyebrow. He had heard countless singers make the same claim. But there was something about Elvis that intrigued him. He asked Elvis to sing.

Elvis took a deep breath and began to sing. His voice filled the room, raw and powerful. It was a mix of country, blues, and gospel, a sound that was both familiar and completely new. Phillips was stunned. He had never heard anything like it before.

"Sing it again," Phillips demanded.

Elvis sang again, this time with even more passion. When he finished, there was silence in the room. Then, Sam Phillips smiled. He knew he had found something special.

"We're gonna make a record," Phillips said, his eyes gleaming with excitement.

Those words changed Elvis's life forever. He had finally found his place in the world. Sun Records was his home, and Sam Phillips was his mentor. The journey to becoming the King of Rock and Roll had begun.

Recording His First Hits

The day Elvis walked into Sun Records with his guitar was a turning point. Sam Phillips knew he had discovered something special, a raw talent with the potential to change the world. The recording sessions that followed were filled with excitement, creativity, and a touch of magic.

Scotty Moore, a brilliant guitarist, and Bill Black, a steady-handed bassist, joined Elvis in the studio. Together, they created a sound that was unlike anything the world had ever heard before. It was a mix of country, blues, and rhythm and blues, with a raw energy that was pure electric.

Their first recording session was a blur of excitement. Elvis sang with a passion that was infectious. Scotty and Bill played with a tight, driving rhythm that pushed the music forward. Sam Phillips stood in the control room, his eyes wide with amazement. He knew he was witnessing something extraordinary.

Their first single, "That's All Right Mama," was a revelation. It was a simple song, but Elvis's voice and the band's energy transformed it into something explosive. When the record hit the airwaves, it was like a bolt of lightning. People were captivated by the raw, rebellious sound.

"That's All Right Mama" was followed by other hits like "Blue Suede Shoes" and "Hound Dog." Each song was a testament to

Elvis's talent and the magic that happened when he, Scotty, and Bill played together.

Elvis was becoming a star, but it wasn't easy. There were long hours in the studio, endless rehearsals, and the constant pressure to deliver. But Elvis loved every minute of it. He was living his dream.

"The studio was my playground," Elvis would say. "I could experiment, make mistakes, and learn. It was the best time of my life."

As Elvis's popularity grew, so did the expectations. People wanted to know who this young, charismatic singer was. They wanted to know where he came from and what made him tick. The pressure was immense, but Elvis handled it with grace and determination.

He remained grounded, despite the fame and fortune that was coming his way. He never forgot his roots, and he always stayed true to himself. Elvis was more than just a singer; he was a symbol of rebellion, a voice for the young generation.

His music spoke to people on a deep level. It resonated with their hopes, dreams, and frustrations. Elvis was the soundtrack to their lives.

The journey had just begun, but Elvis was already leaving an indelible mark on the world. He was a star on the rise, and nothing could stop him.

CHAPTER 3:

HEARTBREAK HOTEL AND BEYOND

Elvis was a shooting star, and his fame was growing brighter by the day. His records were selling like hotcakes, and people couldn't get enough of his electrifying performances. But with fame came a new set of challenges.

One of Elvis's biggest hits was a song called "Heartbreak Hotel." It was a song about loneliness and heartbreak, and Elvis poured his heart and soul into it. The song connected with millions of people who felt lost and alone. It was like Elvis was singing their story.

"Heartbreak Hotel" was more than just a song; it was a phenomenon. People were captivated by Elvis's raw emotion and his ability to connect with his audience on a deep level. He was no longer just a singer; he was a symbol of a generation.

Elvis's success caught the attention of RCA Victor, a major record label. They saw the potential in this young, charismatic star and offered him a record deal. It was a big step for Elvis, but he was ready for the challenge.

With RCA Victor, Elvis had the resources to take his career to the next level. He recorded a series of hit songs, including "Hound Dog," "Love Me Tender," and "Don't Be Cruel." These songs cemented his status as the King of Rock and Roll.

But fame came with a price. Elvis was constantly in the spotlight, and his personal life was under scrutiny. People were fascinated by his every move, and the pressure to maintain a perfect image was immense.

Elvis tried to stay grounded, but it wasn't easy. He missed the simple life he had once known. The constant travel, the endless interviews, and the demands of his fans took a toll on him.

Despite the challenges, Elvis continued to create amazing music. He experimented with different genres, from rock and roll to ballads. He was a chameleon, able to adapt to any style and make it his own.

Elvis's live performances were legendary. He had an undeniable stage presence, and his energy was infectious. Fans went wild when they saw him perform, and his concerts became the stuff of legend.

The world was at Elvis's feet, but he never forgot where he came from. He remained loyal to his friends and family, and he used his platform to help others. He was a role model for millions of young people, and his influence would be felt for generations to come.

The Ed Sullivan Show

Elvis had captured the hearts of millions with his records, but it was television that would truly make him a household name. The Ed Sullivan Show was the biggest and most popular show on television, and it was the ultimate stage for any aspiring star.

Getting booked on the Ed Sullivan Show was a huge deal. It was like winning the lottery.

But even for Elvis, with his growing popularity, it wasn't a sure thing. Ed Sullivan was known for his conservative values, and some of Elvis's moves were considered too provocative for television.

There was a lot of controversy surrounding Elvis's appearance on the show. Some people thought he was too wild and rebellious, while others couldn't get enough of him. But one thing was for sure, the anticipation was building to a fever pitch.

When Elvis finally appeared on the Ed Sullivan Show, it was like a bomb going off.

America had never seen anything like it before. Elvis's charisma, his voice, and his electrifying stage presence captivated the nation. People were glued to their television screens, mesmerized by the young man with the golden voice.

His performance of "Hound Dog" was legendary. As he moved his hips and shook his body, the camera focused on his waistline. The image was censored, but it only fueled the public's fascination. People were talking about Elvis for days, weeks, even months after his appearance.

The Ed Sullivan Show turned Elvis into a national sensation. He was no longer just a singer; he was a cultural icon. His impact on popular culture was undeniable. He had broken down barriers and changed the way people thought about music and television.

After his appearance on the Ed Sullivan Show, Elvis became a household name. He was invited to appear on other television shows, and his records continued to sell like crazy. He was the biggest star in the world, and it seemed like nothing could stop him.

But with great fame comes great responsibility. Elvis was constantly in the spotlight, and the pressure to maintain his image was immense. He struggled to balance his personal life with his public persona.

Despite the challenges, Elvis remained true to himself. He continued to make great music and perform electrifying shows. He was a pioneer, a trailblazer, and a true original.

The Ed Sullivan Show was just the beginning for Elvis. His journey was far from over.

The Elvis Phenomenon

Elvis wasn't just a singer; he was like a super-cool superhero who could make everyone happy with his music! When he sang, it was like magic. People would dance, clap, and shout with joy. It was like a big party every time he performed.

Elvis had a special way of moving his body. He'd shake his hips and swing his arms, and everyone would copy him. It was like a dance craze that swept the whole country!

Kids, grown-ups, even grandparents were doing the "Elvis Presley" moves.

People loved Elvis's clothes too. He dressed in shiny suits with fancy belts and big sunglasses. He looked so cool that everyone wanted to dress like him. Stores started selling clothes just like Elvis wore, and kids begged their parents to buy them.

Elvis's songs were like stories with happy endings. They were about love, heartbreak, and having fun. Everyone could relate to his songs, no matter how old they were. You could be feeling sad, but as soon as you heard Elvis sing, you'd start to feel better.

His voice was like a rainbow, with colors that could make you laugh, cry, or dream. He could sing slow, dreamy songs that made you feel like you were floating on a cloud, or he could sing fast, upbeat songs that made you want to jump up and dance.

Elvis was more than just a singer. He was a symbol of hope and happiness. He showed people that dreams could come true, and that anyone could be a star. He was like a shining light in the darkness, and people were drawn to his warmth and kindness.

That's why they called him the King. He ruled everyone's hearts with his music and his amazing personality. Elvis was a legend, and his music will live on forever.

CHAPTER 4: MOVIES, MUSIC, AND MILITARY SERVICE

From Singer to Actor

Elvis was a superstar, but even superstars have to try new things. Hollywood came calling, and soon, Elvis was trading his microphone for a movie camera. It was like stepping into a whole new world, full of lights, cameras, and fancy costumes.

At first, Elvis was excited about acting. He admired actors like Marlon Brando and James Dean, and he wanted to show the world that he could be more than just a singer. He wanted to be taken seriously as an actor.

His first movie was called "Love Me Tender," and it was a big hit. People loved seeing Elvis on the big screen, singing and dancing and looking handsome. But as time went on, the movie roles started to get a bit samey. It was always the same story: Elvis plays a cool guy who sings a bunch of songs and falls in love with a pretty girl.

While Elvis was making lots of money and his fans loved the movies, he started to feel a little bored. He wanted to do something different, something that would challenge him as an actor. But the movie studio wanted to keep making the same kind of movies, because they were making a lot of money.

It was a tough spot to be in. Elvis wanted to grow as an actor, but the studio wanted to keep him in the same old box. It was like being a really good basketball player, but only being allowed to shoot free throws.

Even though the movies weren't always the best, Elvis still had fun making them. He loved meeting new people, learning new things, and of course, singing and dancing. And let's face it, he looked pretty cool in all those fancy outfits!

Serving His Country

Imagine being the biggest star in the world and suddenly having to trade your fancy clothes for an army uniform. That's what happened to Elvis! It was a big surprise for everyone, but Elvis was a good guy and he knew it was his duty to serve his country.

Leaving behind the glitz and glamour of Hollywood wasn't easy. Elvis missed performing and being in the spotlight. But he also felt proud to be serving his country. He wanted to prove to everyone that he was more than just a pretty face.

Basic training was tough. Elvis had to wake up early, march in formation, and learn how to shoot a gun. It was a world away from the life he was used to. But Elvis was determined to be the best soldier he could be. He wanted to make his family and his country proud.

After basic training, Elvis was sent to Germany. It was a big adventure, and he loved exploring the country. He even learned to speak a little German! But Elvis was still a big star, and people recognized him everywhere he went. It was hard to have a normal life when everyone wanted a piece of you.

Even though Elvis was in the army, he never stopped making music. He would play guitar for his fellow soldiers, and they loved it. He even recorded a few songs while he was in Germany.

When Elvis finished his military service, he came back to America a changed man. He had grown up and matured. He was ready to take on the world again.

Coming Back Stronger

When Elvis returned from the army, the world was a different place. Rock and roll had changed, and so had the music industry. But Elvis was ready for the challenge. He was back, and he was stronger than ever.

His first TV special, the "Elvis Comeback Special," was a huge hit. It showed the world that Elvis was still the King. He sang classic rock and roll songs, but he also performed some new, more experimental material. It was a bold move, but it paid off. The special was a ratings smash, and it re-established Elvis as a relevant and exciting artist.

After the comeback special, Elvis embarked on a series of successful tours. He played to packed stadiums, and his fans went wild. It was like he had never been away. But the constant touring was exhausting, and Elvis started to feel the strain.

He tried to find a balance between his personal life and his career, but it was difficult. The pressure to be perfect was immense, and it took a toll on his health. Elvis turned to prescription drugs as a way to cope with the stress, a habit that would eventually lead to serious problems.

Despite the challenges, Elvis continued to make music. He released a string of hit albums and singles, and he experimented with different genres. He was a true artist, always searching for new sounds and new ways to express himself.

But as the 1970s progressed, Elvis's health began to decline. The weight of fame and the toll of his lifestyle were taking their toll. He retreated to his home in Graceland, where he found solace in his music and his family.

Even in his final years, Elvis continued to create beautiful music. His voice may have lost some of its power, but his passion and emotion remained intact. He was a legend, and he knew it.

Elvis Presley died on August 16, 1977, but his legacy lives on. He is remembered as one of the greatest entertainers of all time, a cultural icon who changed the world. His music continues to inspire and delight people of all ages.

The King is dead, long live the King!

Chapter 5:

The Las Vegas Era

Elvis was tired of being on the road. Traveling from city to city was exhausting, and he missed his home in Graceland. So, he decided to try something new: Las Vegas!

Las Vegas was a shiny, sparkly city, full of lights and excitement. It was like a grown-up playground, with casinos, shows, and fancy hotels. Elvis thought it would be the perfect place to put on a big show and entertain his fans.

When Elvis stepped onto the stage in Las Vegas, it was like magic. The crowd went wild! He wore sparkly suits and sang his heart out. He danced and joked, and everyone loved it. Elvis was the King of Rock and Roll, but in Las Vegas, he became the King of the Stage.

His shows were like big parties. People came from all over to see him perform. They sang along to his songs, laughed at his jokes, and danced in the aisles. It was like one giant, happy family.

Elvis loved performing in Las Vegas. He had a lot of fun, and he made a lot of money. But it wasn't all glitz and glamor. The pressure to put on a great show every night was huge. Elvis was a perfectionist, and he wanted to give his fans the best show possible.

Sometimes, the late nights and the bright lights took their toll. Elvis struggled with his health, and he turned to prescription drugs to help him cope. It was a dangerous path, but he couldn't seem to break free.

Even though Elvis was facing challenges, he continued to be a superstar. He was loved by millions, and his music brought joy to people all over the world. Las Vegas was his kingdom, and he ruled it with style and grace.

A Glittering Lifestyle

Las Vegas was a world of glitz and glamor, and Elvis lived right in the middle of it. He stayed in the fanciest hotels, wore the most expensive suits, and drove the coolest cars. It was like living in a dream.

Elvis loved to surround himself with beautiful things. He had a huge collection of cars, motorcycles, and airplanes. He loved to go shopping, and he had a closet full of amazing clothes. His home, Graceland, was a palace filled with treasures from all over the world.

But all that glitz and glamor came with a price. Elvis was lonely. He was surrounded by people, but he felt alone. He missed the simple life he had once known. He longed for the days when he could just hang out with his friends and family without being in the spotlight.

Elvis tried to find happiness in his personal life, but it was difficult. He got married a few times, but none of the relationships lasted. He was searching for something real, something genuine, but it seemed to always be just out of reach.

Despite his personal struggles, Elvis continued to perform. He loved being on stage, and he loved making his fans happy. But the pressure to be perfect was taking its toll. He was exhausted, both physically and emotionally.

Elvis turned to prescription drugs to help him cope with the stress. It was a dangerous habit, but he couldn't seem to break free. The drugs were a way to escape the pain, but they were also a prison.

A Timeless Talent

Even though Elvis was going through a tough time, his talent never faded. He was still the King of Rock and Roll, and his fans loved him more than ever. His Las Vegas shows were legendary, and people came from all over the world to see him perform.

Elvis had an incredible stage presence. He could command an audience like no one else. When he stepped onto the stage, it was like magic. He would sing with such passion and energy that it would electrify the crowd. And his voice? It was still as powerful and beautiful as ever.

Elvis was more than just a singer. He was a showman. He loved to entertain, and he knew how to connect with his audience. He would tell jokes, flirt with the ladies, and even do a little karate. It was like watching a one-man circus.

But behind the glitz and glamour, Elvis was a man who was struggling. He was trying to find himself, to find a sense of peace and purpose. He was searching for something real, something lasting.

Despite his personal challenges, Elvis continued to make music. He recorded new albums, and he experimented with different styles. He was always looking for ways to grow as an artist.

Elvis's music was timeless. It touched people of all ages and backgrounds. His songs were anthems of love, loss, and longing. They were songs that people could relate to, songs that would stay with them forever.

Even as his health declined, Elvis continued to perform. He was a fighter, and he wasn't going to let anything stop him. He loved his fans, and he wanted to give them everything he had.

CHAPTER 6: THE LEGACY LIVES ON

The King's Farewell

Elvis was tired. His heart was heavy, and his body was worn out. The glitz and glamour of Las Vegas had lost its shine. He missed his home, his family, and the simple life he once knew.

One day, Elvis's heart stopped beating. It was a sad day for the whole world. People were heartbroken. They couldn't believe that the King was gone. But even though Elvis wasn't here anymore, his music lived on.

His songs were like stars in the night sky, shining bright and beautiful. People still danced to his music, sang along to his lyrics, and dreamed of the day they would see him again.

Elvis's home, Graceland, became a special place. People from all over the world came to visit, to feel closer to the King. They walked through his house, saw his clothes, and imagined what life was like for him.

Elvis left behind a big legacy. He changed the world with his music, his style, and his spirit. He showed us that dreams can come true, and that anything is possible if you believe in yourself.

Even though Elvis is gone, his music lives on. It's like a time machine that takes us back to a happier time. It makes us smile, dance, and feel good.

Elvis was more than just a singer. He was a friend, a hero, and a king. And he will always be remembered as the greatest entertainer of all time.

Elvis: A Global Icon

Elvis Presley was more than just an American star; he was a global icon. His music, his style, and his charisma captivated people from all corners of the world. From the bustling cities of Europe to the far-off lands of Asia, Elvis left an enduring mark on popular culture.

In countries like England, Germany, and France, Elvis mania swept the nation. Young people dressed like him, danced to his music, and dreamed of meeting him. His concerts were sold-out events, and his records topped the charts.

Elvis's influence extended beyond the Western world. In countries like Japan, Australia, and Brazil, he was adored by millions. His music was a universal language that transcended cultural barriers.

Even today, decades after his death, Elvis's legacy continues to grow. New generations of fans are discovering his music, and they are just as captivated as their parents and grandparents were.

Elvis Presley was a one-of-a-kind talent, a true original. He changed the world with his music, and his impact will be felt for generations to come.

Keeping the Music Alive

Elvis's music was a gift that kept on giving. Even after his death, his songs continued to touch people's hearts. New generations discovered his music, and they fell in love with it just as much as their parents and grandparents had.

Elvis's legacy inspired countless musicians. Artists from all genres, from rock and roll to country to pop, have cited Elvis as a major influence. His unique blend of styles and his powerful stage presence have shaped the music industry for decades.

To keep Elvis's memory alive, many tribute artists have emerged. These talented performers dedicate their careers to honoring Elvis's music and his iconic image. They bring his spirit to new audiences, ensuring that his legacy continues to shine.

Graceland, Elvis's beloved home, has become a pilgrimage site for fans from around the world. It's a place where people can connect with Elvis's spirit and feel closer to their idol. The mansion has been preserved as a museum, allowing visitors to step into Elvis's world and experience his life.

Elvis Presley's music is a timeless treasure. It transcends generations and cultures. His legacy is a testament to the power of music to unite people and bring joy to the world.

Glossary: Music Terms

Beat: The basic pulse of music. It's like the steady heartbeat of a song.

Chorus: The most memorable part of a song, often repeated. It's the part you're likely to sing along to.

Melody: The tune of a song, the part you whistle or hum.

Rhythm: The pattern of sounds in music. It's what makes you tap your foot or clap your hands.

Verse: A section of a song that tells a story or sets a mood.

Chorus: The part of a song that's repeated, often the catchiest part.

Bridge: A section of a song that connects the verses and chorus, often adding a new melody or harmony.

Tempo: The speed of a song. A fast tempo makes you feel energetic, while a slow tempo can be relaxing.

Dynamics: How loud or soft the music is. Soft parts are called "piano," and loud parts are called "forte."

Harmony: The way different notes sound together. It's like the colors that make up a beautiful picture.

Blues: A type of music that often expresses sadness or longing. It's known for its soulful sound.

Rock and Roll: A type of music that combines elements of blues, country, and rhythm and blues. It's energetic and exciting.

Gospel: A type of religious music that is often powerful and inspiring.

Country: A type of music that tells stories about life in the countryside. It's often associated with guitars and fiddles.

Rhythm and Blues: A type of music that combines elements of blues and jazz. It's known for its soulful vocals and rhythmic grooves.

Elvis-related Vocabulary

- **Graceland:** Elvis Presley's iconic home in Memphis, Tennessee.
- **Rockabilly:** A genre of music that combines elements of rock and roll, country, and rhythm and blues, popularized by Elvis Presley.
- **Heartbreak Hotel:** One of Elvis Presley's most famous songs.
- **Hound Dog:** Another iconic Elvis Presley song.

- **Blue Suede Shoes:** A popular Elvis Presley song and a fashion trend.

- **Jailhouse Rock:** An energetic Elvis Presley song and movie.

- **King of Rock and Roll:** A nickname given to Elvis Presley.

- **Memphis Mafia:** Elvis Presley's close circle of friends and associates.

- **Aloha from Hawaii:** A famous television special starring Elvis Presley.

- **G.I. Blues:** An Elvis Presley movie set during his military service.

- **Viva Las Vegas:** An Elvis Presley movie and song associated with his Las Vegas residency.
- **Hound Dog:** A nickname sometimes given to Elvis Presley.

Elvis Dance Moves

Elvis Presley wasn't just a great singer; he was also a fantastic dancer! His moves were so cool that everyone wanted to copy him. Let's learn some of his famous dance steps:

The Hip Shake

This was Elvis's signature move. Stand with your feet shoulder-width apart and bend your knees slightly. Now, slowly move your hips from side to side in a circular motion. Add some arm movements for extra flair!

The Pelvis Twist

This move is all about the lower body. Stand with your feet together and bend your knees slightly. Twist your hips from side to side, keeping your upper body still.

The Cowboy Strut

Elvis loved to strut his stuff on stage. Stand tall and proud, and take big, confident steps. Swing your arms slightly as you walk, and imagine you're the coolest person in the room!

The Graceland Glide

This is a smoother move. Glide across the floor, shifting your weight from one foot to the other. Keep your body relaxed and your movements flowing.

Remember, the most important thing is to have fun! Put on your favorite Elvis song and let your body move to the rhythm. You might even come up with your own Elvis-inspired dance moves!

Quiz Time!

1. In what city was Elvis Presley born?

- a) Memphis, Tennessee
- b) Tupelo, Mississippi
- c) Nashville, Tennessee
- d) New Orleans, Louisiana

2. What was the name of Elvis Presley's first big hit song?

- a) Heartbreak Hotel
- b) Hound Dog
- c) Blue Suede Shoes
- d) Jailhouse Rock

3. What was the name of Elvis Presley's famous home?

- a) Graceland
- b) Whitehaven Mansion
- c) Sun Studio
- d) Beverly Hills Palace

4. What was the name of Elvis Presley's iconic dance move?

- a) The Twist
- b) The Monkey
- c) The Hip Shake
- d) The Moonwalk

5. Which U.S. military branch did Elvis Presley serve in?

- a) Army
- b) Navy
- c) Air Force
- d) Marines

6. In which city did Elvis Presley have a famous Las Vegas residency?

- a) Atlantic City
- b) New York City
- c) Los Angeles
- d) Las Vegas

7. What was the nickname given to Elvis Presley?

- a) The King of Rock and Roll
- b) The King of Pop
- c) The Voice
- d) The Idol

8. Which instrument did Elvis Presley primarily play?

- a) Piano
- b) Guitar
- c) Drums
- d) Saxophone

9. What was the name of Elvis Presley's iconic movie where he played a rebellious teenager?
   - a) Jailhouse Rock
   - b) Blue Hawaii
   - c) Viva Las Vegas
   - d) Love Me Tender

10. What was the name of the record label where Elvis Presley recorded his early hits?
    - a) RCA Records
    - b) Columbia Records
    - c) Motown Records
    - d) Sun Records

Quiz Answers

1. **b) Tupelo, Mississippi**
2. **a) Heartbreak Hotel**
3. **a) Graceland**
4. **c) The Hip Shake**
5. **a) Army**
6. **d) Las Vegas**
7. **a) The King of Rock and Roll**
8. **b) Guitar**
9. **a) Jailhouse Rock**
10. **d) Sun Records**

Made in the USA
Columbia, SC
04 November 2024